T0198976

The Copper Christmas Pig

Written by Carolyn Straub

Illustrations by Hanna Stephenson

This book is a work of non-fiction. Unless otherwise noted, the author and the publisher make no explicit guarantees as to the accuracy of the information contained in this book and in some cases, names of people and places have been altered to protect their privacy.

WestBow Press books may be ordered through booksellers or by contacting:

WestBow Press
A Division of Thomas Nelson & Zondervan
1663 Liberty Drive
Bloomington, IN 47403
www.westbowpress.com
1 (866) 928-1240

Because of the dynamic nature of the Internet, any web addresses or links contained in this book may have changed since publication and may no longer be valid. The views expressed in this work are solely those of the author and do not necessarily reflect the views of the publisher, and the publisher hereby disclaims any responsibility for them.

Any people depicted in stock imagery provided by Getty Images are models, and such images are being used for illustrative purposes only. Certain stock imagery © Getty Images.

Illustrations by Hanna Stephenson.

Scripture quotations taken from The Holy Bible, New International Version® NIV® Copyright © 1973 1978 1984 2011 by Biblica, Inc. TM. Used by permission. All rights reserved worldwide.

ISBN: 978-1-9736-7686-7 (sc)
ISBN: 978-1-9736-7687-4 (e)

Library of Congress Control Number: 2019915774

Print information available on the last page.

WestBow Press rev. date: 10/17/2019

WESTBOW
PRESS®
A DIVISION OF THOMAS NELSON
& ZONDERVAN

Dedication

To Traci and Jillayne,

Who lived this story

and

For children of all ages,

who dream, pray and trust

Acknowledgements

Heartfelt thanks to my~

Son, Cameron Straub for technical illustrations

Husband, Dan Straub for faithful encouragement

Fellow Interrobang authors' edits and

suggestions

And most of all, to our Loving God for

    Providing everything we need and

    Surprising us with many of our wants!

"Look Mommy! We have *tons* of money this year!" Copper coins rained down from six-year-old Jill's wriggling fingers. The pennies tinkled like bells as they joined the pile on the table.

Nine-year-old Trace gathered them together, forming a shiny mountain beside the empty copper piggy bank.

Trace and Jill's mother worked at a ladies' clothing store. She thanked God every day, for her job and for her family. On paydays, she first set aside money for their offering at church. After that, she paid the bills. Very little money was left for extras, like pizza or movies.

"We'll be fine," she said. "The Bible tells us, 'The Lord provides for his people.' God loves us, and promises to give us everything we need. And He *always* does."

All year long, they saved their pennies in the copper piggy bank that sat on top of their refrigerator. Each December, those pennies paid for their fresh-cut Christmas tree.

"It takes one hundred pennies to make a dollar," Mom reminded them. "But this does look like more than we've had before. Let's get busy and count them. Then we'll know."

Jill and Trace counted and stacked the pennies. Their mother slid the stacks into pink paper rolls of fifty pennies each.

Trace counted the rolls. "Eight dollars and fifty cents. This *is* more!" He pictured their house with the most beautiful Christmas decorations. "Maybe we can buy a tree that's taller than I am. One that stands on the floor!"

"Yes! And we'll have the biggest and best birthday party for Jesus ever!" Jill said, clapping her hands. "I'm going to pray for that!"

Mom thought, *that would be wonderful, all right. Dear Lord,* she prayed silently, *you know my kids are good kids. They don't ask for much.*

But is a fabulous Christmas tree something we **need***?*

Please help us be to be grateful for whatever tree we can afford. Amen.

Wearing their warm jackets and gloves, Trace, Jill and Mom piled into Babe, their baby blue Volkswagen Beetle.

Off they went in search of a bargain.

Not far from home was the Oregon Tree Lot. Every year, a wrinkled little man arrived in a rusty, old, yellow Oregon school bus. The bus was stuffed to the ceiling with fresh-cut trees.

This was their favorite Christmas tree lot. But "Mr. Oregon" had hundreds of customers. He didn't remember them from year to year.

"These trees smell so good, Mom, like at that campground in the mountains," Trace said.

Slowly they walked, searching for the best tree. In the third row they spotted an Austrian pine with long, fine needles and a perfect shape.

They turned the tree around, carefully inspecting it. It looked excellent. But it had no price tag.

Mom found Mr. Oregon and asked how much it cost. She returned to Trace and Jill, who waited by the tree.

"I'm sorry kids, this one costs $13.75. It's way over our budget. Let's keep looking."

Sadly, they wandered on, eyeing every tree. But none compared to that expensive Austrian pine.

"Uh-oh, Trace. Where's Jill?" Mom sounded scared. Little sister was nowhere to be seen.

"Jill, Jill," they called as they rushed back, checking every row.

Finally, they found her, exactly where they last saw her. There she stood, with feet firmly planted. Her sturdy arms were locked around that Austrian pine, while a man and woman tried their best to examine the tree. They, too, had heard the price of $13.75.

The more the couple talked about purchasing the tree, the tighter Jill squeezed it. She closed her eyes. Was she talking to God? The couple walked away.

Mom had never seen Jill behave like this. She knelt beside her and whispered, "We can't buy this tree, Sweetie. We don't have enough money."

"But this is OUR tree, Mommy!" Jill whimpered. I just *know* it is." Hot tears spilled quietly down Jill's cold, red cheeks and she hugged the tree closer.

Embarrassed by his sister's behavior, Trace wished he could find a place to hide.

The couple returned. "Lady, are you buying it or not?" the man asked gruffly. "Because if you don't, we will."

They moved a short distance away and waited.

Without warning, Mr. Oregon's lined face popped forth from his green-needle forest.

"Pssst!" he whispered to Mom. "You can have that tree for $8.50."

Eight-fifty? Mom thought. *How could he know exactly how much money we have? Did God speak to Mr. Oregon?*

Hearing shrieks of laughter, Trace rushed to join them in a bouncing hug. "Thank you, Lord!"

But when Mom pulled the coin rolls out to pay Mr. Oregon, Trace's joy quickly vanished. His face turned beet red. "Mother!" he whispered. "Couldn't you have changed the pennies into MONEY? I can't believe you're paying with penny rolls! What will people think of us?"

Before Mom could remind Trace that this was their tradition, he hurried off to wait by the car.

Tying the big bushy tree onto Babe was a major job. It almost covered the Beetle. Their heads could barely be seen through the windows, as the little car crept slowly back home.

After church on Christmas Eve, they celebrated at their traditional open house.

Trace, Jill and Mom told everyone the story of how God, again, provided all of their needs—plus a perfect Christmas tree for Jesus's birthday!

All the guests agreed it was an outstanding tree, and that God had, indeed, blessed them all.

From high atop the refrigerator, the copper pig listened to their joyous celebration and smiled.

He was already collecting pennies for next year's tree shopping adventure.

Possible Chat Points With Your Child

There are many things we want, but what are some things that we NEED?

How has God provided your needs?

When have you prayed for something special?

How has God surprised you?

Let's thank God for taking good care of us.

Matt. 6:8; Matt. 18:2-4; Phil. 4:19

Printed in the United States
By Bookmasters